Contents

MW01715396

Introduction

The fate of the free world hangs each day on the attentiveness and skill of the United States Secret Service. They protect the president and other high government officials from people who are always watching for weaknesses they can exploit to cause harm and wreak havoc.

How many Secret Service officers do you know by name? It's probably the same number as that of the royal cupbearers and food tasters you can remember from history. The fact is, most people don't go down in history for doing their job well. Yet the foundation of the next generation is laid with our hard work and skillful service today.

Nehemiah was the royal cupbearer to the king of Persia, the chief world power of that time. The cupbearer was a servant, and yet his integrity was critical. His job was to detect any poison in his master's drink before it was served. Yet Nehemiah was a servant leader whose strength of character went far beyond the norm, and who eventually made a difference in world history.

Like Nehemiah, we all have important jobs to do, and as long as we do a pretty good job most of us go relatively unnoticed. But, also like Nehemiah, God has put us in a strategic position according to a larger plan. What will keep us ready for the watershed decisions of our lives, for the pivotal events? How will we stay focused as we face frequent discouragement and opposition? What will keep us going when we lose sight of the big picture and are consumed with the daily grind?

These seven studies give clear principles for cupbearers—for us average people who nonetheless want to make a difference in our families and communities. We want to set an example that might nourish the next generation when times are tough. We want to be genuinely successful in a way that won't be erased by the sands of time.

May God bless your step of faith as you study these biblical principles; may God make them come alive for you.

DISCOVER**LIFE**

Success for the Asking

Lesson 1

Nehemiah 1:1-4

[1]The words of Nehemiah son of Hacaliah:

In the month of Kislev in the twentieth year, while I was in the citadel of Susa, [2]Hanani, one of my brothers, came from Judah with some other men, and I questioned them about the Jewish remnant that survived the exile, and also about Jerusalem.

[3]They said to me, "Those who survived the exile and are back in the province are in great trouble and disgrace. The wall of Jerusalem is broken down, and its gates have been burned with fire."

[4]When I heard these things, I sat down and wept. For some days I mourned and fasted and prayed before the God of heaven.

Nehemiah 1:5-11

Then I said:

"O LORD, God of heaven, the great and awesome God, who keeps his covenant of love with those who love him and obey his commands, [6]let your ear be attentive and your eyes open to hear the prayer your servant is praying before you day and night for your servants, the people of Israel. I confess the sins we Israelites, including myself and my father's house, have committed against you. [7]We have acted very wickedly toward you. We have not obeyed the commands, decrees and laws you gave your servant Moses.

[8]"Remember the instruction you gave your servant Moses, saying, 'If you are unfaithful, I will scatter you among the nations, [9]but if you return to me and obey my commands, then even if your exiled people are at the farthest horizon, I will gather them from there and bring them to the place I have chosen as a dwelling for my Name.'

[10]"They are your servants and your people, whom you redeemed by your great strength and your mighty hand. [11]O Lord, let your ear be attentive to the prayer of this your servant and to the prayer of your servants who delight in revering your name. Give your servant success today by granting him favor in the presence of this man."

I was cupbearer to the king.

Nehemiah 2:1-6

[1]In the month of Nisan in the twentieth year of King Artaxerxes, when wine was brought for him, I took the wine and gave it to the king. I had not been sad in his presence before; [2]so the king asked me, "Why does your face look so sad when you are not ill? This can be nothing but sadness of heart."

I was very much afraid, [3]but I said to the king, "May the king live forever! Why should my face not look sad when the city where my fathers are buried lies in ruins, and its gates have been destroyed by fire?"

[4]The king said to me, "What is it you want?"

Then I prayed to the God of heaven, [5]and I answered the king, "If it pleases the king and if your servant has found favor in his sight, let him send me to the city in Judah where my fathers are buried so that I can rebuild it."

[6]Then the king, with the queen sitting beside him, asked me, "How long will your journey take, and when will you get back?" It pleased the king to send me; so I set a time.

Nehemiah 2:7-10

[7]I also said to him, "If it pleases the king, may I have letters to the governors of Trans-Euphrates, so that they will provide me safe-conduct until I arrive in Judah? [8]And may I have a letter to Asaph, keeper of the king's forest, so he will give me timber to make beams for the gates of the citadel by the temple and for the city wall and for the residence I will occupy?" And because the gracious hand of my God was upon me, the king granted my requests. [9]So I went to the governors of Trans-Euphrates and gave them the king's letters. The king had also sent army officers and cavalry with me.

[10]When Sanballat the Horonite and Tobiah the Ammonite official heard about this, they were very much disturbed that someone had come to promote the welfare of the Israelites.

Questions

1. **If you could ask for one major change in your country or community or family, what would you ask for?**
2. **Nehemiah 1:1-4**
   a. What does Hanani report concerning Jerusalem?
   b. How does Nehemiah react to the news, and what does that tell us about him?
3. **Nehemiah 1:5-11**
   a. How does Nehemiah address God?
   b. What does Nehemiah confess?
   c. What promise does Nehemiah claim, and why?
   d. What does he ask for himself?
   e. What does a cupbearer or food taster for royalty actually do?
4. **Nehemiah 2:1-6**
   a. Would you consider Nehemiah fearful or bold? Why?
   b. How does God give Nehemiah the success he had prayed for?
   c. What insight do we gain into Nehemiah's prayer life from verse 4?
5. **Nehemiah 2:7-10**
   a. How does Nehemiah show forethought and careful planning?
   b. How does Nehemiah account for the king's consent to his request?
   c. What hostile reaction does Nehemiah encounter?

STUDIES IN THIS SERIES

Lesson 1: Success for the Asking
Lesson 2: They Had Their Backs to a Wall
Lesson 3: How to be Good and Mad
Lesson 4: When Push Comes to Shove
Lesson 5: They Found Joy in a Book
Lesson 6: God Gives His People Joy
Lesson 7: The Danger of Compromise

afterWord

Fewer Leaders, Greater Expectations

While the pool of workers in business and industry continues to shrink, the job of the leader grows more demanding as business changes at an accelerating rate and leaders have to juggle more duties, according to William Byham, president and CEO of Development Dimensions International, a human resources and training consulting firm.

"The jump bar is going up, and there are more bars," says Byham. "We're running into it all the time in our company. We're partnering with a company and also competing with them. It gets complicated."

Mergers, acquisitions, expansions, and organizational restructurings are coming at a faster rate. Meanwhile, businesses are venturing into the global marketplace, so leaders have to be able to adjust to other cultures and transcend geographic boundaries.

"You have to be skilled in more things, and you have to be better in each of those areas," says Byham, author of a dozen books on management.

—*SMALL BUSINESS NEWS PITTSBURGH,* MARCH 2000

The Measure of Greatness

Here is how Jesus turned the power scale upside-down. Greatness is measured by taking the last place, by a total commitment to welcome the "little ones," by a breadth of sympathy and an openness to all who name his name, by a passion for personal purity, by toughness with ourselves but gentleness with others. Here are the questions he gives to measure our greatness:

Not "How many people help me?" but "How *deep* is my commitment to others?"

Not "Whom do I let into the circle of influence?" but "How *long* and *broad* is my circle of fellowship? Whom can I include and still be loyal to Jesus?"

Not "How can I best develop myself?" but "How *intense* is my passion to be pure and useful?"

—LEIGHTON FORD IN *TRANSFORMING LEADERSHIP* (INTERVARSITY PRESS)

What Will Others Think?

If Jesus Christ had taken a poll, he would never have preached the gospel.

—U.S. REP. HENRY HYDE ON ABC-TV'S "THIS WEEK" (12/13/98)

A Fresh Look at Prayer

I used to write in my daily calendar, "7:00-7:30 a.m.: Prayer." But many times I passed that up. It was one more thing to pass by that day. Now I write "7:00-7:30 a.m.: God."

Somehow that's a little harder to neglect.

—JOHN RICHES IN *CHRISTIAN SPIRITUALITY: THEMES FROM THE TRADITION* (PAULIST PRESS)

To answer prayer is God's universal rule. . . . God's Word does not say, "Call unto me, and you will thereby be trained into the happy art of knowing how to be denied. Ask, and you will learn sweet patience by getting nothing." Far from it. But it is definite, clear and positive: "Ask, and it shall be given unto you."

—E. M. BOUNDS

Success and Failure

For slightly more than thirty years Erma Bombeck wrote her humor column. During that time, she published fifteen books, was recognized as one of the twenty-five most influential women in America, appeared frequently on the television show *Good Morning America,* was featured on the cover of *Time* magazine, received innumerable honors (such as the American Cancer Society's Medal of Honor), and was awarded fifteen honorary degrees. But during that span of time, Erma Bombeck also experienced incredible troubles and trials including breast cancer, a mastectomy, and kidney failure. And she wasn't shy about sharing her perspective on her life experiences:

> I speak at college commencement, and I tell everyone I'm up here and they're down there, not because of my successes, but my failures. Then I proceed to spin all of them off—a comedy record album that sold two copies in Beirut . . . a sitcom that lasted about as long as a donut in our house . . . a Broadway play that never saw Broadway . . . a book signing where I attracted two people: one who wanted directions to the restroom and the other who wanted to buy the desk.
>
> What you have to tell yourself is, "I'm not a failure. I failed at doing something." There's a big difference. . . . Personally and career-wise, it's been a corduroy road. I've buried babies, lost parents, had cancer, and worried over kids. The trick is to put it all in perspective . . . and that's what I do for a living.

—JOHN C. MAXWELL IN *FAILING FORWARD* (THOMAS NELSON PUBLISHERS)

Focus on What Matters Most

Each morning I make a W.A.M.M. (What Activities Matter Most?) list. I need crystal clarity on what's important and what's peripheral.

Peter Drucker writes that recognizing what counts as a true contribution is the great challenge for people in work like ours. If I don't do this, it's embarrassing to me how much time I can waste.

Sloth, Frederick Beuchner said, isn't necessarily incompatible with heavy activity. It's failing to do what needs to be done when it needs to be done. Like the kamikaze pilot who flew seventeen missions.

—JOHN ORTBERG IN *LEADERSHIP*

DISCOVERLIFE

They Had Their Backs to a Wall

Lesson 2

Nehemiah 2:11-13, 16

[11]I went to Jerusalem, and after staying there three days [12]I set out during the night with a few men. I had not told anyone what my God had put in my heart to do for Jerusalem. There were no mounts with me except the one I was riding on.

[13]By night I went out through the Valley Gate toward the Jackal Well and the Dung Gate, examining the walls of Jerusalem, which had been broken down, and its gates, which had been destroyed by fire.

[16]The officials did not know where I had gone or what I was doing, because as yet I had said nothing to the Jews or the priests or nobles or officials or any others who would be doing the work.

Nehemiah 2:17-20

[17]Then I said to them, "You see the trouble we are in: Jerusalem lies in ruins, and its gates have been burned with fire. Come, let us rebuild the wall of Jerusalem, and we will no longer be in disgrace." [18]I also told them about the gracious hand of my God upon me and what the king had said to me.

They replied, "Let us start rebuilding." So they began this good work. [19]But when Sanballat the Horonite, Tobiah the Ammonite official and Geshem the Arab heard about it, they mocked and ridiculed us. "What is this you are doing?" they asked. "Are you rebelling against the king?"

[20]I answered them by saying, "The God of heaven will give us success. We his servants will start rebuilding, but as for you, you have no share in Jerusalem or any claim or historic right to it."

Nehemiah 4:1-6

[1]When Sanballat heard that we were rebuilding the wall, he became angry and was greatly incensed. He ridiculed the Jews, [2]and in the presence of his associates and the army of Samaria, he said, "What are those feeble Jews doing? Will they restore their wall? Will they offer sacrifices? Will they finish in a day? Can they bring the stones back to life from those heaps of rubble—burned as they are?"

[3]Tobiah the Ammonite, who was at his side, said, "What they are building—if even a fox climbed up on it, he would break down their wall of stones!"

[4]Hear us, O our God, for we are despised. Turn their insults back on their own heads. Give them over as plunder in a land of captivity. [5]Do not cover up their guilt or blot out their sins from your sight, for they have thrown insults in the face of the builders.

[6]So we rebuilt the wall till all of it reached half its height, for the people worked with all their heart.

Nehemiah 4:7-15

[7]But when Sanballat, Tobiah, the Arabs, the Ammonites and the men of Ashdod heard that the repairs to Jerusalem's walls had gone ahead and that the gaps were being closed, they were very angry. [8]They all plotted together to come and fight against Jerusalem and stir up trouble against it. [9]But we prayed to our God and posted a guard day and night to meet this threat.

[10]Meanwhile, the people in Judah said, "The strength of the laborers is giving out, and there is so much rubble that we cannot rebuild the wall."

[11]Also our enemies said, "Before they know it or see us, we will be right there among them and will kill them and put an end to the work."

[12]Then the Jews who lived near them came and told us ten times over, "Wherever you turn, they will attack us."

[13]Therefore I stationed some of the people behind the lowest points of the wall at the exposed places, posting them by families, with their swords, spears and bows. [14]After I looked things over, I stood up and said to the nobles, the officials and the rest of the people, "Don't be afraid of them. Remember the Lord, who is great and awesome, and fight for your brothers, your sons and your daughters, your wives and your homes." [15]When our enemies heard that we were aware of their plot and that God had frustrated it, we all returned to the wall, each to his own work.

Nehemiah 4:16-22

[16]From that day on, half of my men did the work, while the other half were equipped with spears, shields, bows and armor. The officers posted themselves behind all the people of Judah [17]who were building the wall. Those who carried materials did their work with one hand and held a weapon in the other, [18]and each of the builders wore his sword at his side as he worked. But the man who sounded the trumpet stayed with me.

[19]Then I said to the nobles, the officials and the rest of the people, "The work is extensive and spread out, and we are widely separated from each other along the wall. [20]Wherever you hear the sound of the trumpet, join us there. Our God will fight for us!"

[21]So we continued the work with half the men holding spears, from the first light of dawn till the stars came out. [22]At that time I also said to the people, "Have every man and his helper stay inside Jerusalem at night, so they can serve us as guards by night and workmen by day."

Questions

1. **Do you agree or disagree with this statement: "A certain amount of opposition is a great help to a man"? Explain your answer.**

2. **Nehemiah 2:11-13, 16**
   a. Whose plan is it to rebuild the walls of Jerusalem (v. 12)?

   b. What is the first step in Nehemiah's rebuilding project?

(continued on next page)

STUDIES IN THIS SERIES

3. Nehemiah 2:17-20

a. What reasons does Nehemiah give for rebuilding the walls of Jerusalem?

b. How do neighboring leaders try to discourage Nehemiah and the people?

c. Why was Nehemiah confident of success?

4. Nehemiah 4:1-6

a. How do Sanballat and Tobiah try to discourage the work?

b. How does Nehemiah fight back?

c. How do the people respond after hearing their enemies' criticism and Nehemiah's prayer?

5. Nehemiah 4:7-15

a. Describe Nehemiah's double response to his enemies' plan (v. 9).

b. What threatened the project at that point (vv. 10-12)?

c. What countermoves does Nehemiah make?

d. How is God involved? Do you think the builders would have succeeded without God's help?

6. Nehemiah 4:16-22

a. Describe the "alert plan" Nehemiah put into effect as the work continued.

b. What do we learn about Nehemiah from chapter 4?

*after*Word

God's Will for My Life

Early in my college experience I was praying about God's will for my life. In a flash I saw the future laid out before me: I would transfer from my secular college to Moody Bible Institute and study for the ministry. I would also marry the girl I was dating.

Thrilled at the prospect, I began to praise the Lord. The plan was perfect—with one exception. No one seemed to have informed Moody Bible Institute. A few months after submitting my application, I received a polite letter of rejection. The girl I was "supposed" to marry soon transferred to another school and began dating someone else.

God is infallible in all he says or does and never makes an error in judgment. The same cannot be said of us. We must test any sense of prompting we feel by the clear teaching of God's Word. The Scriptures are always the foundation in matters of guidance and should never be overruled by other sources. God will never prompt us to act contrary to his Word.

Yet many of the decisions we make involve choices between options clearly within the bounds of God's Word. In such cases, being "led of the Spirit" may not be a matter of deciding whom we should marry or which job we should take, as much as one of recognizing the potential for Spirit-empowered obedience to the clear directives of God's Word. How we act once we have made the choice between two equally sanctioned options is often more important than the choice itself.

Certainly, God is concerned about the everyday decisions we must make. He cares about our decision to work at McDonalds over Burger King, or our choice of marrying Jane rather than Joan. But when Romans 8:14 speaks of being "led by the Spirit of God," it refers to our responsibility to put to death the old nature and walk in the new nature (see Rom. 8:13-14). When Paul speaks of being "led" by the Spirit and "keeping in step" with the Spirit, he is calling believers to demonstrate the fruit of the spirit instead of indulging in the deeds of the flesh (Gal. 5:18, 23-25).

Our opportunities to say "no" to the flesh and "yes" to the Spirit may not be as glamorous as the kind of decisions we usually associate with divine guidance, but they happen every day. They are reflected in a mother's choice to forgive rather than hold on to bitterness when she is hurt by one of her family members. An employee chooses the path marked out by God's Spirit when he refuses to engage in workplace gossip. A church member is being led by the Spirit when he notices someone struggling with sin and uses God's Word to restore him (see Gal. 6:1).

—JOHN KOESSLER IN *MOODY*, MARCH/APRIL 2000

Courage

Give us grace, O God, to do the deed which we well know cries out to be done. Let us not hesitate because of ease, or the words of men's mouths, or our own lives. Mighty causes are calling us. . . . But they call with voices that mean work and sacrifice and death. Mercifully grant us, O God, the spirit of Esther, that we say, "I will go unto the King, and if I perish, I perish." Amen.

—W. E. B. DUBOIS, A FOUNDER OF THE NAACP

The truth of the matter is that you always know the right thing to do. The hard part is doing it.

—GEN. H. NORMAN SCHWARZKOPF

Prayer Is Work

Prayer is not the foe of work, it does not paralyze activity. It works mightily. . . . It springs activity, stimulates desire and effort. Prayer is not an opiate but a tonic, it does not lull to sleep but arouses anew for action. The lazy man does not, will not, cannot pray, for prayer demands energy.

—E. M. BOUNDS

DISCOVER**LIFE**

How to Be Good and Mad

Lesson 3

Nehemiah 5:1-5

1Now the men and their wives
raised a great outcry against their
Jewish brothers. 2Some were saying,
"We and our sons and daughters are
numerous; in order for us to eat and
stay alive, we must get grain."

3Others were saying, "We are
mortgaging our fields, our vineyards
and our homes to get grain during
the famine."

4Still others were saying, "We have
had to borrow money to pay the
king's tax on our fields and vine-
yards. 5Although we are of the same
flesh and blood as our countrymen
and though our sons are as good as
theirs, yet we have to subject our sons
and daughters to slavery. Some of our
daughters have already been en-
slaved, but we are powerless, because
our fields and our vineyards belong
to others."

Nehemiah 5:6-11

6When I heard their outcry and
these charges, I was very angry. 7I
pondered them in my mind and then
accused the nobles and officials. I
told them, "You are exacting usury
from your own countrymen!" So I
called together a large meeting to
deal with them 8and said: "As far as
possible, we have bought back our
Jewish brothers who were sold to the
Gentiles. Now you are selling your
brothers, only for them to be sold
back to us!" They kept quiet, because
they could find nothing to say.

9So I continued, "What you are
doing is not right. Shouldn't you
walk in the fear of our God to avoid
the reproach of our Gentile enemies?
10I and my brothers and my men are
also lending the people money and
grain. But let the exacting of usury
stop! 11Give back to them immedi-
ately their fields, vineyards, olive
groves and houses, and also the
usury you are charging them—the
hundredth part of the money, grain,
new wine and oil."

Nehemiah 5:12-13

12"We will give it back," they said.
"And we will not demand anything
more from them. We will do as you
say."

Then I summoned the priests and
made the nobles and officials take an
oath to do what they had promised.
13I also shook out the folds of my robe
and said, "In this way may God
shake out of his house and posses-
sions every man who does not keep
this promise. So may such a man be
shaken out and emptied!"

At this the whole assembly said,
"Amen," and praised the LORD. And
the people did as they had promised.

Nehemiah 5:14-19

14Moreover, from the twentieth
year of King Artaxerxes, when I was
appointed to be their governor in the
land of Judah, until his thirty-second
year—twelve years—neither I nor
my brothers ate the food allotted to
the governor. 15But the earlier gover-
nors—those preceding me—placed a
heavy burden on the people and took
forty shekels of silver from them in
addition to food and wine. Their
assistants also lorded it over the peo-
ple. But out of reverence for God I
did not act like that. 16Instead, I
devoted myself to the work on this
wall. All my men were assembled
there for the work; we did not
acquire any land.

17Furthermore, a hundred and
fifty Jews and officials ate at my table,
as well as those who came to us from
the surrounding nations. 18Each day
one ox, six choice sheep and some
poultry were prepared for me, and
every ten days an abundant supply of
wine of all kinds. In spite of all this, I
never demanded the food allotted to
the governor, because the demands
were heavy on these people.

19Remember me with favor, O my
God, for all I have done for these peo-
ple.

Questions

1. **When is it OK to be angry?**

2. **Nehemiah 5:1-5**
   a. What problems among the Jews trigger an outcry?
   b. What are the underlying causes of the problem?

3. **Nehemiah 5:6-11**
   a. How does Nehemiah respond to this outcry?
   b. After considering the issue, who does Nehemiah say is the source of the problems?
   c. What solution does Nehemiah propose?

4. **Nehemiah 5:12-13**
   a. What do the nobles and officials do to correct the situation?
   b. What was the point of the oath?

5. **Nehemiah 5:14-19**
   a. Compare Nehemiah's style of leadership with those who preceded him.
   b. If Nehemiah had led like the governors before him, how might the nation's situation have been different?
   c. What evidence is there in this chapter that God cared for the oppressed people?

STUDIES IN THIS SERIES

*after*Word

Answering the Critics

Mike, one of our elders, suggested that we put on paper all the criticisms we had heard and address them head on. We listed all the questions and accusations that we could think of, including the ones we deemed ridiculous. Had we asked people to leave the church? Was the leadership team power hungry? Was the pastor doing the thinking for the elder board? Were we against charismatics?

Since we were only days away from our annual congregational meeting, we decided to make time on the agenda for the list of questions—with answers.

I started the meeting with a nervous stomach. "Most of you know that some families have recently left our church. (I listed their names.) You have heard stories which have likely raised serious questions in your mind. You may have assumed that since we have made no public statement that everything is secret, but this is not the case. This evening I want to discuss openly concerns that may be on your hearts."

There was dead silence in the room. As I proceeded down the list of concerns and criticisms, I could tell people were on board, although they were surprised at our candor. As I continued, people began to relax and sit deeper into their seats. Smiles broke out at some of the questions. When finished, I held my breath, prayed to myself, then asked if there were any additional questions. I wondered if a dam of accusations would break out. Again, there was silence. A peaceful silence.

At the end of the meeting, many people came forward to affirm the leaders for being forthright. I went to bed that evening knowing that a possible division in the congregation in the congregation had been put to rest. Time has proven us right. And trust in our leadership team has increased.

—LANNY KILGORE IN *LEADERSHIP,* SPRING 2000

He Did One Thing Well

Once renowned evangelist Dwight L. Moody entered into a personal relationship with the Lord Jesus Christ, he increasingly became committed—some said obsessively committed—to fulfilling the Great Commission. Indeed, when he overheard the British evangelist Henry Varley say that the world has yet "to see what the Lord can do with a man wholly consecrated to Christ," Moody determined to be that man. He allowed nothing to stand in the way.

Because the drive to rescue lost souls and equip a new generation of Christian workers was so strong in Moody, he made every imaginable effort to avoid getting bogged down in secondary issues.

Like effective evangelists throughout history, this Massachusetts-born preacher refused to take sides on divisive doctrines such as God's sovereignty versus human responsibility, or any one of a host of other issues that mark various denominations.

No one could draw Moody into debates over the merits of one mode of baptism over another. This charitable seeker of lost souls always advocated ministering with people of all denominations as long as they professed love for the Lord Jesus Christ and exhibited a desire to make Him known.

—LYLE W. DORSETT IN *MOODY,* NOVEMBER/DECEMBER 1999

Leaders, Lose the Ego

The real power of leadership lies in servanthood. Damien, the missionary to the lepers of Hawaii, had no resources to speak of, yet he appeared rich. He committed himself to the malformed and dying. In those he served, he wakened an ability to transcend themselves. His selflessness caused the hopeless to care less about their own suffering than they did about the needs of others. Damien gave such dignity to the dying that he brought the word *hope* back to their vocabulary. He proved that servant leadership is never a saucer where surface and depth lie close together. Leadership is rather a well where the substance of the soul lies deep and its well rope is long to reach the cold, pure depths.

What denotes servant leadership? A strange unawareness of ego. Servant leaders are task-centered. Because they tend to pick great tasks, they always feel overwhelmed and inadequate. Because they feel inadequate, they seek to look beyond themselves for answers. They don't do this to be heroic. They do it to be honest. They know they don't have all the answers.

Their commitment to the task means that real leaders . . . know that hiring strong associates helps them eliminate the weaknesses in their organization. Strong organizations are more important to them than egoistic reputations. They crave a strong organization above a good image. They deplore incompetency, even when incompetents by contrast point up their strengths. Their feeling of weakness has a wonderful spiritual dimension. Feelings of inadequacy in Christian leaders cause them to compensate for their weaknesses by turning inwardly to Christ.

—CALVIN MILLER IN *THE EMPOWERED LEADER* (BROADMAN & HOLMAN PUBLISHERS, 1995)

Servant Leadership

Biblical servant leadership has paradoxical qualities. Leaders have the courage to make decisions on behalf of the group, when group well-being is endangered. But the leadership privileges normally associated with status, ego, financial gain, and a lust for power have been replaced by servanthood attitudes.

—STAN PLETT

DISCOVER**LIFE**

When Push Comes to Shove

Lesson 4

Nehemiah 6:1-4

[1]When word came to Sanballat, Tobiah, Geshem the Arab and the rest of our enemies that I had rebuilt the wall and not a gap was left in it—though up to that time I had not set the doors in the gates—[2]Sanballat and Geshem sent me this message: "Come, let us meet together in one of the villages on the plain of Ono."

But they were scheming to harm me; [3]so I sent messengers to them with this reply: "I am carrying on a great project and cannot go down. Why should the work stop while I leave it and go down to you?" [4]Four times they sent me the same message, and each time I gave them the same answer.

Nehemiah 6:5-9

[5]Then, the fifth time, Sanballat sent his aide to me with the same message, and in his hand was an unsealed letter [6]in which was written:

"It is reported among the nations—and Geshem says it is true—that you and the Jews are plotting to revolt, and therefore you are building the wall. Moreover, according to these reports you are about to become their king [7]and have even appointed prophets to make this proclamation about you in Jerusalem: 'There is a king in Judah!' Now this report will get back to the king; so come, let us confer together."

[8]I sent him this reply: "Nothing like what you are saying is happening; you are just making it up out of your head."

[9]They were all trying to frighten us, thinking, "Their hands will get too weak for the work, and it will not be completed."

[But I prayed,] "Now strengthen my hands."

Nehemiah 6:10-14

[10]One day I went to the house of Shemaiah son of Delaiah, the son of Mehetabel, who was shut in at his home. He said, "Let us meet in the house of God, inside the temple, and let us close the temple doors, because men are coming to kill you—by night they are coming to kill you."

[11]But I said, "Should a man like me run away? Or should one like me go into the temple to save his life? I will not go!" [12]I realized that God had not sent him, but that he had prophesied against me because Tobiah and Sanballat had hired him. [13]He had been hired to intimidate me so that I would commit a sin by doing this, and then they would give me a bad name to discredit me.

[14]Remember Tobiah and Sanballat, O my God, because of what they have done; remember also the prophetess Noadiah and the rest of the prophets who have been trying to intimidate me.

Nehemiah 6:15-19

[15]So the wall was completed on the twenty-fifth of Elul, in fifty-two days. [16]When all our enemies heard about this, all the surrounding nations were afraid and lost their self-confidence, because they realized that this work had been done with the help of our God.

[17]Also, in those days the nobles of Judah were sending many letters to Tobiah, and replies from Tobiah kept coming to them. [18]For many in Judah were under oath to him, since he was son-in-law to Shecaniah son of Arah, and his son Jehohanan had married the daughter of Meshullam son of Berekiah. [19]Moreover, they kept reporting to me his good deeds and then telling him what I said. And Tobiah sent letters to intimidate me.

Nehemiah 7:1-3

[1]After the wall had been rebuilt and I had set the doors in place, the gatekeepers and the singers and the Levites were appointed. [2]I put in charge of Jerusalem my brother Hanani, along with Hananiah the commander of the citadel, because he was a man of integrity and feared God more than most men do. [3]I said to them, "The gates of Jerusalem are not to be opened until the sun is hot. While the gatekeepers are still on duty, have them shut the doors and bar them. Also appoint residents of Jerusalem as guards, some at their posts and some near their own houses."

STUDIES IN THIS SERIES

Questions

1. **What is the best thing a person can do when facing a danger or threat?**
2. **Nehemiah 6:1-4**
   a. What new tactics do Nehemiah's enemies try?
   b. What keeps Nehemiah from being lured into their trap?
3. **Nehemiah 6:5-9**
   a. Why might Sanballat have left the letter unsealed?
   b. What is the gist of Nehemiah's reply to Sanballat?
   c. Where does Nehemiah get his courage?
4. **Nehemiah 6:10-14**
   a. How does Shemaiah try to ensnare Nehemiah?
   b. How does Nehemiah respond to Shemaiah's tactics?
   c. What does Nehemiah's response reveal about his character?
   d. What does Nehemiah ask of God?
5. **Nehemiah 6:15-19**
   a. How was such a gigantic task completed in such a short time, despite troubles from without and within?
   b. How do the surrounding nations respond to the news that the wall has been completed?
   c. What problems continue to plague Nehemiah after the wall is finished?
6. **Nehemiah 7:1-3**
   a. What three groups are first appointed after the wall is completed?
   b. Who is put in charge?
   c. What instructions does Nehemiah give?

afterWord

Keeping the Right Focus

During construction of Emerson Hall at Harvard University, president Charles Eliot invited psychologist and philosopher William James to suggest a suitable inscription for the stone lintel over the doors of the new home of the philosophy department.

After some reflection, James sent Eliot a line from the Greek philosopher Protagoras: "Man is the measure of all things."

James never heard back from Eliot, so his curiosity was piqued when he spotted artisans working on a scaffold hidden by a canvas. One morning, the scaffold and canvas were gone. The inscription? "What is man that thou art mindful of him?"

Eliot had replaced James's suggestion with words from the Psalmist. Between these two lines lies the great distance between the God-centered and the human-centered points of view.

—WARREN BIRD IN *LEADERSHIP,* SPRING 1997

Keeping Perspective

Failure is an inside job. So is success. If you want to achieve, you have to win the war in your thinking first. You can't let the failure outside you get inside you. You certainly can't control the length of your life—but you can control its width and depth. You can't control the contour of your face—but you can control its expression. You can't control the weather—but you can control the atmosphere of your mind. Why worry about things you can't control when you can keep yourself busy controlling the things that depend on you?

I read an article that highlighted the strength, courage, and resilience of the Norwegian people. Some of the toughest explorers in history have come from Norway. . . . It doesn't matter how harsh the climate or how difficult the circumstances; they always seem to persevere.

That ability has become a part of their culture. They are a nation of outdoor enthusiasts—living on the edge of the Arctic Circle. The Norwegians have a saying that I think captures their attitude: "There is no such thing as bad weather, only bad clothing."

—JOHN C. MAXWELL IN *FAILING FORWARD* (THOMAS NELSON, 2000)

A man is not defeated by his opponents but by himself.
—JAN CHRISTIAAN SMUTS

Never, Never, Never Give Up

As a young teenager, Sir Winston Churchill attended a public school called Harrow. He was a rambunctious sort and probably would have been expelled had he not been the son of the famed Lord Randolph Churchill. But Sir Winston went on to build a brilliant career in the British military, finally becoming prime minister, leading his nation through the dark days of World War II.

When asked to speak at his old school, Churchill agreed. The schoolmaster gave the prime minister a glowing introduction. The students listened intently to hear what wisdom the greatest leader in their nation would give them. Drawing himself up to his full stature—all five feet, five inches, and 235 pounds of him—Churchill made this brief but unforgettable speech: "Young men, never give up. Never give up! Never give up!! Never, never, never, never!"

How to Handle the Critics

Abraham Lincoln might have broken under the strain of the Civil War if he hadn't learned the folly of trying to answer all the angry criticism hurled at him. His description of how he handled his critics has become a literary gem.

General MacArthur had a copy of it hanging above his headquarters desk during the war; and Winston Churchill kept a framed copy of it on the walls of his study at Chartwell. It goes like this:

"If I were to try to read, much less to answer, all the attacks made on me, this shop might as well be closed for any other business. I do the very best I know how—the very best I can; and I mean to keep on doing so until the end. If the end brings me out all right, then what is said against me won't matter. If the end brings me out wrong, then ten angels swearing I was right would make no difference."

How to Run with Patience

Bob Wieland finally crossed the finish line on Thursday, November 6, 1986, the New York City Marathon's 19,413th and final finisher . . . and the first to run a marathon with his arms instead of his legs! Wieland is a 40-year-old Californian whose legs were blown off in a Vietnam battlefield. He recorded what race officials said was the slowest time in marathon history: four days, two hours, 48 minutes, 17 seconds. But he was greeted like a champion by race director Fred Lebow, who had written Wieland off as a dropout.

When he finished, Wieland claimed his finisher's medal and explained why he did it: "For the same reason as 20,000 other people. It's the greatest marathon in the country." He also cited three specific reasons: to show his born-again Christian faith; to test his conditioning; and to promote the President's Council on Physical Fitness, of which he is a member.

Wieland said, "Success is not based on where you start, it's where you finish, and I finished. The first step was the most difficult, after that, we were on our way home. The joy has been the journey."

—*THE DENVER POST*

DISCOVERLIFE

They Found Joy in a Book

Lesson 5

Nehemiah 8:1-3

[1]When the seventh month came and the Israelites had settled in their towns, all the people assembled as one man in the square before the Water Gate. They told Ezra the scribe to bring out the Book of the Law of Moses, which the LORD had commanded for Israel.

[2]So on the first day of the seventh month Ezra the priest brought the Law before the assembly, which was made up of men and women and all who were able to understand. [3]He read it aloud from daybreak till noon as he faced the square before the Water Gate in the presence of the men, women and others who could understand. And all the people listened attentively to the Book of the Law.

Nehemiah 8:4-8

[4]Ezra the scribe stood on a high wooden platform built for the occasion. Beside him on his right stood Mattithiah, Shema, Anaiah, Uriah, Hilkiah and Maaseiah; and on his left were Pedaiah, Mishael, Malkijah, Hashum, Hashbaddanah, Zechariah and Meshullam.

[5]Ezra opened the book. All the people could see him because he was standing above them; and as he opened it, the people all stood up. [6]Ezra praised the LORD, the great God; and all the people lifted their hands and responded, "Amen! Amen!" Then they bowed down and worshiped the LORD with their faces to the ground.

[7]The Levites—Jeshua, Bani, Sherebiah, Jamin, Akkub, Shabbethai, Hodiah, Maaseiah, Kelita, Azariah, Jozabad, Hanan and Pelaiah—instructed the people in the Law while the people were standing there. [8]They read from the Book of the Law of God, making it clear and giving the meaning so that the people could understand what was being read.

Nehemiah 8:9-12

[9]Then Nehemiah the governor, Ezra the priest and scribe, and the Levites who were instructing the people said to them all, "This day is sacred to the LORD your God. Do not mourn or weep." For all the people had been weeping as they listened to the words of the Law.

[10]Nehemiah said, "Go and enjoy choice food and sweet drinks, and send some to those who have nothing prepared. This day is sacred to our Lord. Do not grieve, for the joy of the LORD is your strength."

[11]The Levites calmed all the people, saying, "Be still, for this is a sacred day. Do not grieve."

[12]Then all the people went away to eat and drink, to send portions of food and to celebrate with great joy, because they now understood the words that had been made known to them.

Nehemiah 8:13-18

[13]On the second day of the month, the heads of all the families, along with the priests and the Levites, gathered around Ezra the scribe to give attention to the words of the Law. [14]They found written in the Law, which the LORD had commanded through Moses, that the Israelites were to live in booths during the feast of the seventh month [15]and that they should proclaim this word and spread it throughout their towns and in Jerusalem: "Go out into the hill country and bring back branches from olive and wild olive trees, and from myrtles, palms and shade trees, to make booths"—as it is written.

[16]So the people went out and brought back branches and built themselves booths on their own roofs, in their courtyards, in the courts of the house of God and in the square by the Water Gate and the one by the Gate of Ephraim. [17]The whole company that had returned from exile built booths and lived in them. From the days of Joshua son of Nun until that day, the Israelites had not celebrated it like this. And their joy was very great.

[18]Day after day, from the first day to the last, Ezra read from the Book of the Law of God. They celebrated the feast for seven days, and on the eighth day, in accordance with the regulation, there was an assembly.

Questions

1. **What would you say to a person who asked, "How can I find joy in my life?"**

2. **Nehemiah 8:1-3**
   a. Describe what happened on the first day of the seventh month.
   b. How do the people respond?

3. **Nehemiah 8:4-8**
   a. How do the people show their readiness to hear the Word of God?
   b. What help do the Levites give?

4. **Nehemiah 8:9-12**
   a. How do the people respond to the reading of the Law?
   b. How are they to celebrate?
   c. What was so significant about the people understanding the words of the Lord?

5. **Nehemiah 8:13-18**
   a. What command do the people find in the Law on the second day of the month?
   b. What do they do about this discovery?
   c. What are the most important things we have discovered from Nehemiah so far?

STUDIES IN THIS SERIES

afterWord

Good News at Work

I find joy in staying after men who need the Lord. I pick some tough targets. I pray for them, spend time with them, share my life with them, and then watch them come to Christ. Nothing pumps my tire like snatching someone from death to life.

I meet a man on his turf. I go to his business office or out to lunch wherever he wants to go. The thing that revs me up for preaching is the real-life working-out of the gospel as it changes the lives of men.

—BUFE KARRAKER IN *LEADERSHIP*, FALL 1998

Do You Know Yourself?

Most of us measure our sinfulness in one of two ways. We count our sins and for most of us, while realizing we are not perfect, we feel we score pretty well. Or we play the comparison game. The sense that we are not as bad as others bolsters our sense of being all right.

Unfortunately, our problem before a Holy God is not the amount of our sins, but the fact that we are sinners. Within us lies the potential for every heinous sin. When a public scandal is exposed, we express moral outrage—never considering that within each of us lies the potential for all of those sins and more. We could be the rapists, the child-abusers, the serial killers of our world. If it weren't for the inexplicable grace of God, they could have very well been us.

Before God, we are no different than the worst of these—we are just forgiven and by grace have been given new desires and opportunities to live for him.

If your relationship with God is about counting your sins, you will find it hard to adore your Savior. But if you realize that it is your sinfulness—not your sins—that nailed him to the tree, then you will never recover from the impact of that kind of mercy in your life. Until we recover an accurate view of ourselves in terms of the reality of our condition before God, we will not know how great his grace is, nor will our hearts acknowledge the debt we owe.

Affectionate adoration is the response of a heart that needs to be—and has been—forgiven much. It ignites from our recognition of the reality of our jeopardy before God and the inexhaustible grace and mercy he has shown us.

—JOSEPH M. STOWELL IN *MOODY*, JANUARY/FEBRUARY 2000

Gifts of Joy

God created two special gifts—laughter and music.

It's been shown that laughter has positive effects on the immune and cardiovascular systems. People who laugh readily get well quicker. So I seek laughter any way I can find it. Laughing at myself is one of the best things I do.

Music has the capacity to go straight through multiple emotional levels and sail right past my defenses. Music massages me at the deepest level. When I'm hurting, sometimes music is the only thing that reaches me, and it reaches me fast. I have no explanation for this except God has ordained it to be so.

Reconciliation brings me joy. I try not to get into situations where I have conflict or enemies, but everybody on the face of the earth does. There is a feeling that comes when you've made your enemy your friend that is unlike anything else.

Doing something creative brings joy to me. I'm sometimes mad at God that he's asked me to be a writer, because it's such hard work. But when I start with a blank sheet of paper and later see what I've written, that brings joy to me. It's the same as mowing my lawn or roto-tilling the garden. There's something about bringing order out of disorder, bringing something out of nothing, accomplishing something worthwhile or beautiful, that at the end of the day brings joy.

Successfully getting rid of things that sabotage my joy brings me joy. When I'm upset about something, and then I'm able to jettison that stuff out of my life, I feel good. I can take a breath of fresh air.

—RICHARD SWENSON IN *LEADERSHIP*, FALL 1998

A Puzzling Verse

Paul tells us in 1 Thessalonians 5:17 to "pray without ceasing." How can we accomplish this essential praying with so many other demands on our time?

Consider that when walking with a loved one, it is not necessary to communicate by talking all the time. I remember times walking with my wife, when for long periods we didn't exchange a word . . . yet the warmth of her hand in mine, her occasional glance, and the aura of her presence served as communication between us that exceeded any words.

That's the way we should walk with God, every minute of every day—aware of his continual presence, although not needing to talk to him every minute.

One way to pray to God throughout your day with him is by echoing the words God has spoken to us through Scriptures we have memorized.

I live in an area surrounded by hills and mountains. When I get the paper in the morning, I look at the gorgeous terrain and repeat Psalm 121, *"I lift up my eyes to the hills—where does my help come from? My help comes from the* LORD, *the Maker of heaven and earth."* What an inspiring way to start the day.

When troubling or inappropriate thoughts start crowding into my mind, I thank God for 2 Corinthians 10:4-5, *"The weapons we fight with are not the weapons of the world. . . . We demolish arguments . . . and we take captive every thought to make it obedient to Christ."*

A dozen times a day, verses of praise, comfort, support, and petition come to mind.

There is no substitute for the Scriptures. A thorough knowledge of the Bible offers us resources beyond our comprehension. If you want to experience the joy of praying without ceasing, memorize God's Word.

—WILLIAM R. NESBITT JR. IN *MOODY*, MARCH/APRIL 2000

DISCOVER*LIFE*

God Gives His People Joy

Lesson 6

Nehemiah 9:1-3

1 On the twenty-fourth day of the same month, the Israelites gathered together, fasting and wearing sackcloth and having dust on their heads. 2 Those of Israelite descent had separated themselves from all foreigners. They stood in their places and confessed their sins and the wickedness of their fathers. 3 They stood where they were and read from the Book of the Law of the LORD their God for a quarter of the day, and spent another quarter in confession and in worshiping the LORD their God.

Nehemiah 9:38

"In view of all this, we are making a binding agreement, putting it in writing, and our leaders, our Levites and our priests are affixing their seals to it."

Nehemiah 10:28-33

28 "The rest of the people—priests, Levites, gatekeepers, singers, temple servants and all who separated themselves from the neighboring peoples for the sake of the Law of God, together with their wives and all their sons and daughters who are able to understand— 29 all these now join their brothers the nobles, and bind themselves with a curse and an oath to follow the Law of God given through Moses the servant of God and to obey carefully all the commands, regulations and decrees of the LORD our Lord.

30 "We promise not to give our daughters in marriage to the peoples around us or take their daughters for our sons.

31 "When the neighboring peoples bring merchandise or grain to sell on the Sabbath, we will not buy from them on the Sabbath or on any holy day. Every seventh year we will forgo working the land and will cancel all debts.

32 "We assume the responsibility for carrying out the commands to give a third of a shekel each year for the service of the house of our God: 33 for the bread set out on the table; for the regular grain offerings and burnt offerings; for the offerings on the Sabbaths, New Moon festivals and appointed feasts; for the holy offerings; for sin offerings to make atonement for Israel; and for all the duties of the house of our God.

Nehemiah 10:35-37, 39

35 "We also assume responsibility for bringing to the house of the LORD each year the firstfruits of our crops and of every fruit tree.

36 "As it is also written in the Law, we will bring the firstborn of our sons and of our cattle, of our herds and of our flocks to the house of our God, to the priests ministering there.

37 "Moreover, we will bring to the storerooms of the house of our God, to the priests, the first of our ground meal, of our [grain] offerings, of the fruit of all our trees and of our new wine and oil. And we will bring a tithe of our crops to the Levites, for it is the Levites who collect the tithes in all the towns where we work.

39 "The people of Israel, including the Levites, are to bring their contributions of grain, new wine and oil to the storerooms where the articles for the sanctuary are kept and where the ministering priests, the gatekeepers and the singers stay. We will not neglect the house of our God."

Nehemiah 12:27-31, 38, 40, 43

27 At the dedication of the wall of Jerusalem, the Levites were sought out from where they lived and were brought to Jerusalem to celebrate joyfully the dedication with songs of thanksgiving and with the music of cymbals, harps and lyres. 28 The singers also were brought together from the region around Jerusalem—from the villages of the Netophathites, 29 from Beth Gilgal, and from the area of Geba and Azmaveth, for the singers had built villages for themselves around Jerusalem. 30 When the priests and Levites had purified themselves ceremonially, they purified the people, the gates and the wall.

31 I had the leaders of Judah go up on top of the wall. I also assigned two large choirs to give thanks. One was to proceed on top of the wall to the right, toward the Dung Gate.

38 The second choir proceeded in the opposite direction. I followed them on top of the wall, together with half the people—past the Tower of the Ovens to the Broad Wall. . . .

40 The two choirs that gave thanks then took their places in the house of God; so did I, together with half the officials. . . .

43 And on that day they offered great sacrifices, rejoicing because God had given them great joy. The women and children also rejoiced. The sound of rejoicing in Jerusalem could be heard far away.

Nehemiah 12:44-45

44 At that time men were appointed to be in charge of the storerooms for the contributions, firstfruits and tithes. From the fields around the towns they were to bring into the storerooms the portions required by the Law for the priests and the Levites, for Judah was pleased with the ministering priests and Levites. 45 They performed the service of their God and the service of purification, as did also the singers and gatekeepers, according to the commands of David and his son Solomon.

Questions

1. **What value is there in making a promise?**
2. **Nehemiah 9:1-3**
   a. Describe what happens at this assembly.
   b. Why do you think so much time is spent reading the Bible and confessing sin?
3. **Nehemiah 9:38; 10:28-33**
   a. What binding agreement do the people make?
   b. What do they promise regarding marriage? Regarding observance of the Sabbath? Regarding giving to the temple?

(continued on next page)

STUDIES IN THIS SERIES

c. What impact would these commitments have upon Jewish social, economic, and religious life?

4. **Nehemiah 10:35-37, 39**
   a. What do the people promise to do?
   b. Where are these gifts brought?

5. **Nehemiah 12:27-31, 38, 40, 43**
   a. What groups of people are brought in for this occasion?
   b. What do the two choirs do?
   c. Why was giving thanks to God so appropriate at this moment?

6. **Nehemiah 12:44-45**
   What was done to restore and sustain temple worship?

afterWord

What Keeps Us Married

Not long ago, I asked Mom and Dad what made their marriage last, and without skipping a beat on his pacemaker, Dad said, "Senility. I wake up each morning and I can't remember who this old girl is. So each day is a new adventure."

"No, I'm serious," I said. The next morning Mom handed me a note. "You wouldn't show this to anyone, would you?" she asked. "I don't want people to think it's the final word on marriage."

At the top of her note, Mom had written: Five Reasons We're Still Together, by Victor and Bernice Callaway. Turns out my parent's wisdom is just too good to keep to myself, so here is a summary of their fifty-seven years of marital experience.

1. **Example.** When we were married, we hardly knew about divorce. I guess everyone at our wedding, including us, fully expected the knot to stay tied. We had watched their marriages. We had seen their faithfulness. We would stay faithful too.
   We realize you won't have that advantage, Son. Some of your closest friends may pack it in. But no matter how dark the road gets, you will find bright examples of faithfulness. And when you can't find examples, you can still be one.
2. **Commitment.** Sometimes I felt like walking out on Dad. And a few times I did. Early in our marriage I occasionally took long walks to get away from him. But I always returned to his loving arms. We made a pledge before God that we would stay committed to each other for life.
3. **Devotions.** Through reading God's Word and praying together almost every night, we learned what God planned and expected for our marriage. We memorized verses that encouraged us to be loving, kind, and honest and to keep on forgiving. We asked God for guidance and he provided it. We prayed for our children and embrace each one of them as gifts from God.
4. **Togetherness.** As a Christian family we stuck together, warts and all. Though we often failed, we are learning to admit wrong and ask for forgiveness. We laughed lots. We cried lots. We talked lots. We worked together and we played together.
5. **Goals.** Since the day we said our vows, our goal has been to walk worthy of the Lord and to keep on walking until we see his face. Sometimes we've fallen flat on our faces. But when that has happened, we've been given grace to get up and claim God's promise: "My Presence will go with you, and I will give you rest" (Ex. 33:14).

Aging brings with it a whole new challenge. It is no flat plateau; sometimes the hills seem steeper and the cliffs more precarious, but we are learning to trust God for what's ahead and to thank him for the abundant and undeserved mercies of the past.

—PHIL CALLAWAY IN *MARRIAGE PARTNERSHIP*, SPRING 2000

One Man's Integrity

After becoming a Christian, Jack Eckerd, founder of the Eckerd drugstore chain, walked through one of his stores and noticed the glossy copies of *Playboy* and *Penthouse* in the magazine rack. Though his stores regularly carried these publications, his new commitment to Christ made him stop and reevaluate the store's policy.

Eckerd had retired from active management, but he called his president to discuss his convictions and urge him to remove the magazines.

The management resisted, since the sales were very profitable. Eckerd himself, as the largest stockholder, would lose money as well, but he was persistent—the magazines must go.

And they went. All 1,700 Eckerd drugstores cleared their racks of *Playboy*, *Penthouse*, and other similar magazines. And Jack Eckerd urged other retail stores to follow suit.

What prompted Eckerd to speak out and change a profitable and widely accepted store policy? When Charles Colson asked him this, he replied simply, "God wouldn't let me off the hook." According to Colson, this is what it means to live under the lordship of Christ—seeing one's life and world through the eyes of the Lord Jesus, and then doing something about it.

—*JUBILEE*

Keeping Promises

Integrity means in part doing what we said we would do. It means sticking to basic values, no matter what. It means wholeness, honesty, incorruptibility.

Integrity is the cornerstone of all sound management. It affects the smallest, most technical details of our work as well as our basic character. It affects promises, goals, the way we steer an organization into the future.

What does it mean to have integrity in management? There are at least four things involved:

- Setting goals (making promises) that can be accomplished
- Putting all one's energy into those goals
- Immediately notifying those to whom commitments have been made if it is clear the commitments cannot be kept
- Trying to understand reasons for failure and what needs to be done to avoid failure in the future

A promise is a holy thing. It involves the integrity of one's character or business. Always remember that integrity includes keeping promises—doing what you said you would do.

—*CHRISTIAN LEADERSHIP LETTER*

DISCOVER*LIFE*

The Danger of Compromise

Lesson 7

Nehemiah 13:4-9

4 Before this, Eliashib the priest had been put in charge of the storerooms of the house of our God. He was closely associated with Tobiah, 5 and he had provided him with a large room formerly used to store the grain offerings and incense and temple articles, and also the tithes of grain, new wine and oil prescribed for the Levites, singers and gatekeepers, as well as the contributions for the priests.

6 But while all this was going on, I was not in Jerusalem, for in the thirty-second year of Artaxerxes king of Babylon I had returned to the king. Some time later I asked his permission 7 and came back to Jerusalem. Here I learned about the evil thing Eliashib had done in providing Tobiah a room in the courts of the house of God. 8 I was greatly displeased and threw all Tobiah's household goods out of the room. 9 I gave orders to purify the rooms, and then I put back into them the equipment of the house of God, with the grain offerings and the incense.

Nehemiah 13:10-14

10 I also learned that the portions assigned to the Levites had not been given to them, and that all the Levites and singers responsible for the service had gone back to their own fields. 11 So I rebuked the officials and asked them, "Why is the house of God neglected?" Then I called them together and stationed them at their posts.

12 All Judah brought the tithes of grain, new wine and oil into the storerooms. 13 I put Shelemiah the priest, Zadok the scribe, and a Levite named Pedaiah in charge of the storerooms and made Hanan son of Zaccur, the son of Mattaniah, their assistant, because these men were considered trustworthy. They were made responsible for distributing the supplies to their brothers.
14 Remember me for this, O my God, and do not blot out what I have so faithfully done for the house of my God and its services.

Nehemiah 13:15-22

15 In those days I saw men in Judah treading winepresses on the Sabbath and bringing in grain and loading it on donkeys, together with wine, grapes, figs and all other kinds of loads. And they were bringing all this into Jerusalem on the Sabbath. Therefore I warned them against selling food on that day. 16 Men from Tyre who lived in Jerusalem were bringing in fish and all kinds of merchandise and selling them in Jerusalem on the Sabbath to the people of Judah. 17 I rebuked the nobles of Judah and said to them, "What is this wicked thing you are doing—desecrating the Sabbath day? 18 Didn't your forefathers do the same things, so that our God brought all this calamity upon us and upon this city? Now you are stirring up more wrath against Israel by desecrating the Sabbath."

19 When evening shadows fell on the gates of Jerusalem before the Sabbath, I ordered the doors to be shut and not opened until the Sabbath was over. I stationed some of my own men at the gates so that no load could be brought in on the Sabbath day. 20 Once or twice the merchants and sellers of all kinds of goods spent the night outside Jerusalem. 21 But I warned them and said, "Why do you spend the night by the wall? If you do this again, I will lay hands on you." From that time on they no longer came on the Sabbath. 22 Then I commanded the Levites to purify themselves and go and guard the gates in order to keep the Sabbath day holy.

Remember me for this also, O my God, and show mercy to me according to your great love.

Nehemiah 13:23-31

23 Moreover, in those days I saw men of Judah who had married women from Ashdod, Ammon and Moab. 24 Half of their children spoke the language of Ashdod or the language of one of the other peoples, and did not know how to speak the language of Judah. 25 I rebuked them and called curses down on them. I beat some of the men and pulled out their hair. I made them take an oath in God's name and said: "You are not to give your daughters in marriage to their sons, nor are you to take their daughters in marriage for your sons or for yourselves. 26 Was it not because of marriages like these that Solomon king of Israel sinned? Among the many nations there was no king like him. He was loved by his God, and God made him king over all Israel, but even he was led into sin by foreign women. 27 Must we hear now that you too are doing all this terrible wickedness and are being unfaithful to our God by marrying foreign women?"

28 One of the sons of Joiada son of Eliashib the high priest was son-in-law to Sanballat the Horonite. And I drove him away from me.

29 Remember them, O my God, because they defiled the priestly office and the covenant of the priesthood and of the Levites.

30 So I purified the priests and the Levites of everything foreign, and assigned them duties, each to his own task. 31 I also made provision for contributions of wood at designated times, and for the firstfruits.

Remember me with favor, O my God.

Questions

1. **It has been said, "All that is required for evil to triumph is for good men to do nothing." Do you agree? Explain your answer.**
2. **Nehemiah 13:4-9**
   a. What does Nehemiah discover upon returning to Jerusalem?
   b. What actions does Nehemiah take, and why?
3. **Nehemiah 13:10-14**
   a. What aspect of temple worship was being neglected?

(continued on next page)

STUDIES IN THIS SERIES

b. How does Nehemiah plan to prevent neglect of the temple in the future?

c. On what grounds does Nehemiah ask to be remembered?

4. Nehemiah 13:15-22

a. Describe the third abuse that Nehemiah discovers.

b. What precautions does Nehemiah take to prevent further abuse of the Sabbath day?

5. Nehemiah 13:23-31

a. What is the fourth problem Nehemiah encounters?

b. How does Nehemiah deal with the offenders?

c. Why does Nehemiah feel so strongly (vv. 26-27)?

d. How does Nehemiah want God to remember the wicked? To remember himself?

6. Overview

a. What did Nehemiah accomplish during this trip to Jerusalem?

b. What lessons can we learn from this passage?

*after*Word

How to Destroy Society

[My morality] is based on Jewish law, which is what Christian law is really based on.

One woman called who was dating a married guy. I said, "You're helping break up his family."

"Well, he's the one breaking the vows," she said.

"You don't think you have a part in breaking the vows?"

"No."

I said, "Thou shalt not covet. Pretend he's her ox."

Dead silence. There was absolutely no way to get around that. When reason and compassion don't work, I pull out the law.

"Now, why do you think that law was given?" I continued.

"Well, I don't know," she said.

"Do you know which commandment it is?"

"No."

I said, "There's a reason for this law. This is part of how we destroy society. Without that law it would mean that somebody listening to this show, once you get this married guy, will think you're fair game. Is that the world you want to live in? Or do you want to live in a world where everybody's moral but you?"

—DR. LAURA SCHLESSINGER
IN *LEADERSHIP*, WINTER 1998

Killing the Conscience

During my college years, I decided it made no sense to stop at red traffic lights when there was clearly no traffic around. So, I began to stop only briefly—just long enough to check for cars—and then proceed. My stops became shorter and shorter, and eventually I was no longer stopping at all. I would simply check out the landscape well in advance and—if no cars were coming—proceed full speed through the red light.

One day something changed all of that.

I was approaching a light in an isolated area where there was rarely traffic even in the busiest of times. I had already checked out the landscape and was near the empty intersection when a car topped the hill to my left. It was too far away to pose any threat, yet it did pose a problem in that it was a police car. I hit the brakes hard and managed to get the car stopped and received no more punishment than a dirty glance.

I've never run a red light since.

It wasn't the police car that scared me enough to stop running red lights. It was what occurred in the seconds between spotting the patrol car and getting the car stopped. In that instant, my foot moved from the gas pedal to the brake pedal, and then *back* to the gas pedal! I did not will my foot to do that; it just did it. And it did it because I looked up at the light and saw red, but saw no immediate oncoming traffic. To my subconscious mind, those circumstances meant proceed—because that is how I had trained my mind to respond. By my ignoring of what had once been a *clear* signal—a red light—that signal was *no longer* clear.

—J. DOUGLAS BURFORD
IN *LEADERSHIP*, SUMMER 1999

What Jesus Hates

Virtually every time we find Jesus angry, the object of his wrath is religious hypocrisy. Jesus consistently condemned the religious leaders for performing external acts of righteousness for the attention of people, while inside their hearts were far from God and full of unrighteousness (Matt. 15:7-9; 23:1-7, 28-29).

They were doing what they thought were good things, but they were doing them for evil reasons. Jesus' anger burned against the hardness of heart in the legalistic Pharisees (Mark 3:5), against officials who had turned the Temple into a robber's den (Mark 11:15-18), and against the scribes and Pharisees who were leading people to destruction by their traditions (Matt. 23:13-28). Centuries before, God declared to Israel, "I hate, I despise your religious feasts; I cannot stand your assemblies" (Amos 5:21). The very activities that should have drawn the people closer to God had been turned into religious showmanship.

We can fall into the same kind of hypocrisy, unless we learn to hate our own phoniness when approaching God. Do we pray and sing to be heard by people—or by God? Do we go through the motions of the Christian life to try to convince others of our godliness—or are we truly attempting to allow God to transform us from the inside out? Do we enforce a strict moral standard with our children, but forget to allow God's love to permeate the relationship?

—MICHAEL J. WILKINS IN *MOODY*,
JANUARY/FEBRUARY 2000

NEHEMIAH: A SERVANT LEADER

Evaluation Questionnaire

As you complete this study, we invite you to fill out this questionnaire to help us evaluate the effectiveness of our materials. Please be candid.

1. What church or denomination are you from?

2. Where did the group meet? How large was the group? What was the average age of your group members?

3. Was this a church group?___ Mostly unchurched?___ A mix of churched and unchurched?___

4. How would you rate the materials?

   Study Guide:

   ___ excellent ___ very good ___ good ___ fair ___ poor

   Leader's Guide:

   ___ excellent ___ very good ___ good ___ fair ___ poor

5. What did you like best about the materials? Did you like the format of the material?

6. What would you do to improve the materials?

7. In general, what was the experience of the group?

8. How can we help you in the future?

Other comments:

(Optional) Your name ____

Address ____

Fold and tape to mail.

Place
Stamp
Here

FAITH ALIVE
2850 KALAMAZOO AVE. SE
GRAND RAPIDS, MI 49560-0300